TO INFINITY AND BEYOND!

Mick Gowar

OXFORD
UNIVERSITY PRESS

OXFORD
UNIVERSITY PRESS

is a department of the University of Oxford.
It furthers the University's objective of excellence in research, scholarship,
and education by publishing worldwide in

Oxford   New York
Auckland   Cape Town   Dar es Salaam   Hong Kong   Karachi
Kuala Lumpur   Madrid   Melbourne   Mexico City   Nairobi
New Delhi   Shanghai   Taipei   Toronto

With offices in

Argentina   Austria   Brazil   Chile   Czech Republic   France   Greece
Guatemala   Hungary   Italy   Japan   Poland   Portugal   Singapore
South Korea   Switzerland   Thailand   Turkey   Ukraine   Vietnam

Oxford is a registered trade mark of Oxford University Press
in the UK and in certain other countries

Text © Mick Gowar 2007

The moral rights of the author have been asserted

Database right Oxford University Press (maker)

First published 2007

All rights reserved. No part of this publication may be reproduced,
stored in a retrieval system, or transmitted, in any form or by any means,
without the prior permission in writing of Oxford University Press,
or as expressly permitted by law, or under terms agreed with the appropriate
reprographics rights organization. Enquiries concerning reproduction
outside the scope of the above should be sent to the Rights Department,
Oxford University Press, at the address above

You must not circulate this book in any other binding or cover
and you must impose this same condition on any acquirer

British Library Cataloguing in Publication Data

Data available

ISBN: 978-0-19-846126-5

15 17 19 20 18 16 14

Printed in China

Paper used in the production of this book is a natural,
recyclable product made from wood grown in sustainable forests.
The manufacturing process conforms to the environmental
regulations of the country of origin

Acknowledgements

The publisher would like to thank the following for permission to reproduce photographs: **p7** Greg Probst/Corbis UK Ltd.; **p10** Nick Carter/National Trust Photographic Library; **p14** George Bernard/Science Photo Library; **p15** Natural History Museum; **p16**t Mark Furness Collection/Mary Evans Picture Library; **p16**b&**17**&**18**&**19**t&b Royal Geographical Society/Alamy; **p21** Bettmann/Corbis UK Ltd.; **p22**&**23** NASA

Cover photograph: Getty/Photographers choice

Illustrations by Hemesh Alles; **p20**;   Peter Bull Art Studio: **p21**, **p22**; Mark Duffin: **p4**t, **p6**, **p8**t, **p12**b/**13**, **p18**; Martin Impey: **p11**, **p14**; David McAllister/NB Illustration: **p4**b, **p5**, **p7**, **p8**b, **p9**, **p12**t, **p15**

Contents

Viking Vinland:
   Land of grapes   4

Francis Drake sails round
   the world   8

Captain Cook's *Endeavour*   12

South with Shackleton   16

"The *Eagle* has landed":
   Apollo 11   20

Glossary, activities
   and index   24

Viking Vinland: Land of grapes 987–1000

Helluland
Eriksfjord
Reykjavik
Vinland

Leif's voyage
Bjarni's voyage

My name is Leif. I am the son of Eric the Red, the chief of the Viking people who live on Greenland. One day, a young seaman named Bjarni came to my father's hall.

He told us how, when he was sailing from Iceland to Greenland, a thick fog came down. For days he drifted across the great ocean, unable to see anything. When the fog lifted he saw land. He knew it wasn't Greenland. It was a new land.

I decided to find Bjarni's new land. I sailed west with 30 companions, but all we found was a bare rocky land we called Helluland. We sailed south and found a beautiful island. The weather was warm and there was rich grazing for our cattle. Inland we found delicious purple berries like grapes. I named the island Vinland after the berries. We built huts, and for a year we lived in Vinland and then sailed home.

Bjarni and Leif had discovered North America.

Their story was told in the two Vinland Sagas. Here is the part of the story where Leif and his men first step ashore on Vinland:

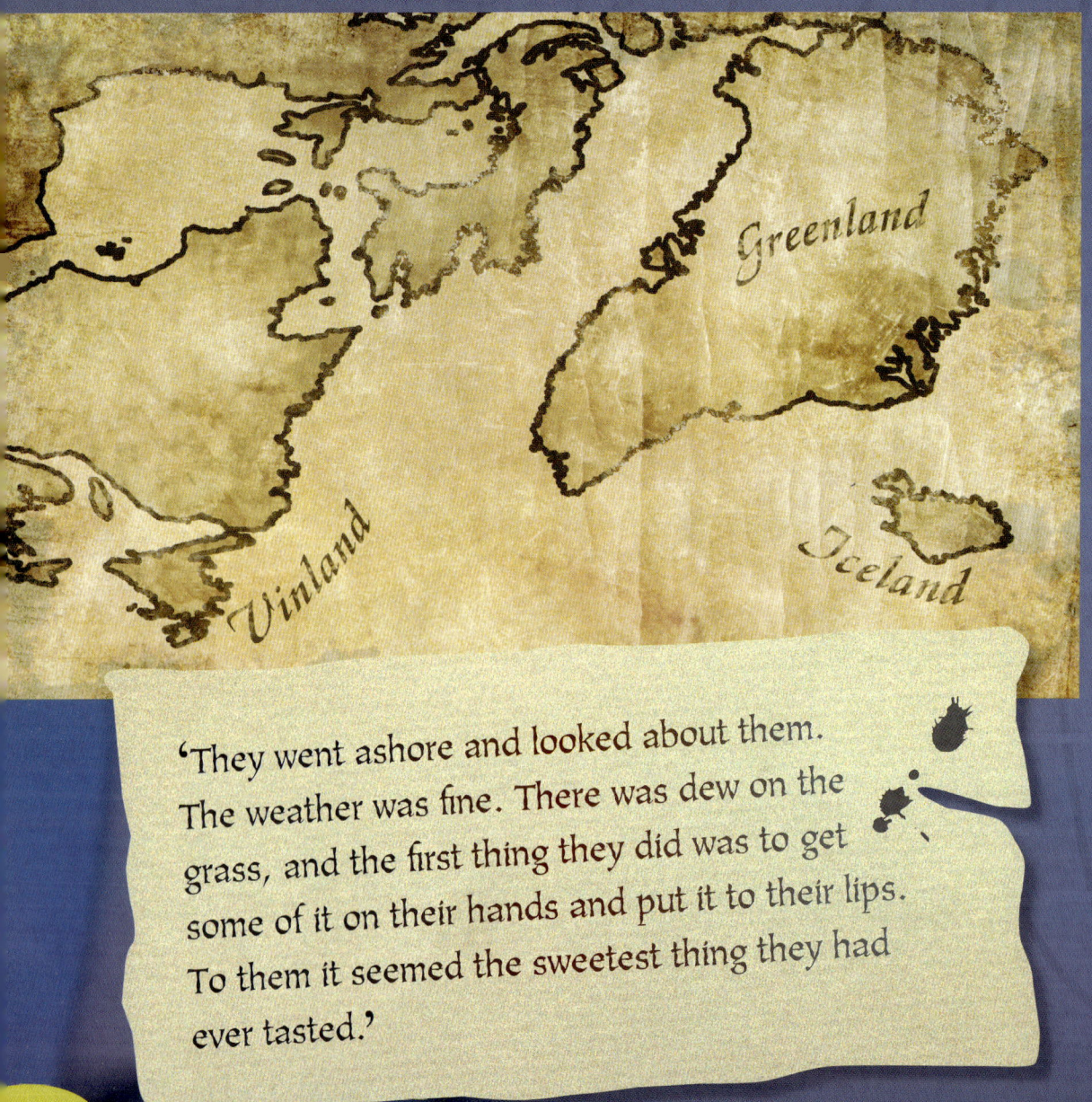

'They went ashore and looked about them. The weather was fine. There was dew on the grass, and the first thing they did was to get some of it on their hands and put it to their lips. To them it seemed the sweetest thing they had ever tasted.'

For many years, people believed that the Vinland Sagas were stories with no basis in fact and that Christopher Columbus was the first European to reach the Americas. But in 1960 archaeologists found the remains of a Viking settlement near the village of L'Anse aux Meadows in Newfoundland, Canada. Some historians believe this was the settlement founded by Leif. It proved that Vikings reached America nearly 500 years before Columbus.

The boats Bjarni and Leif sailed in were called knorrs. They were a new design and excellent for travelling across rough seas. Without knorrs they wouldn't have been able to sail to Vinland.

Francis Drake sails round the world 1577–80

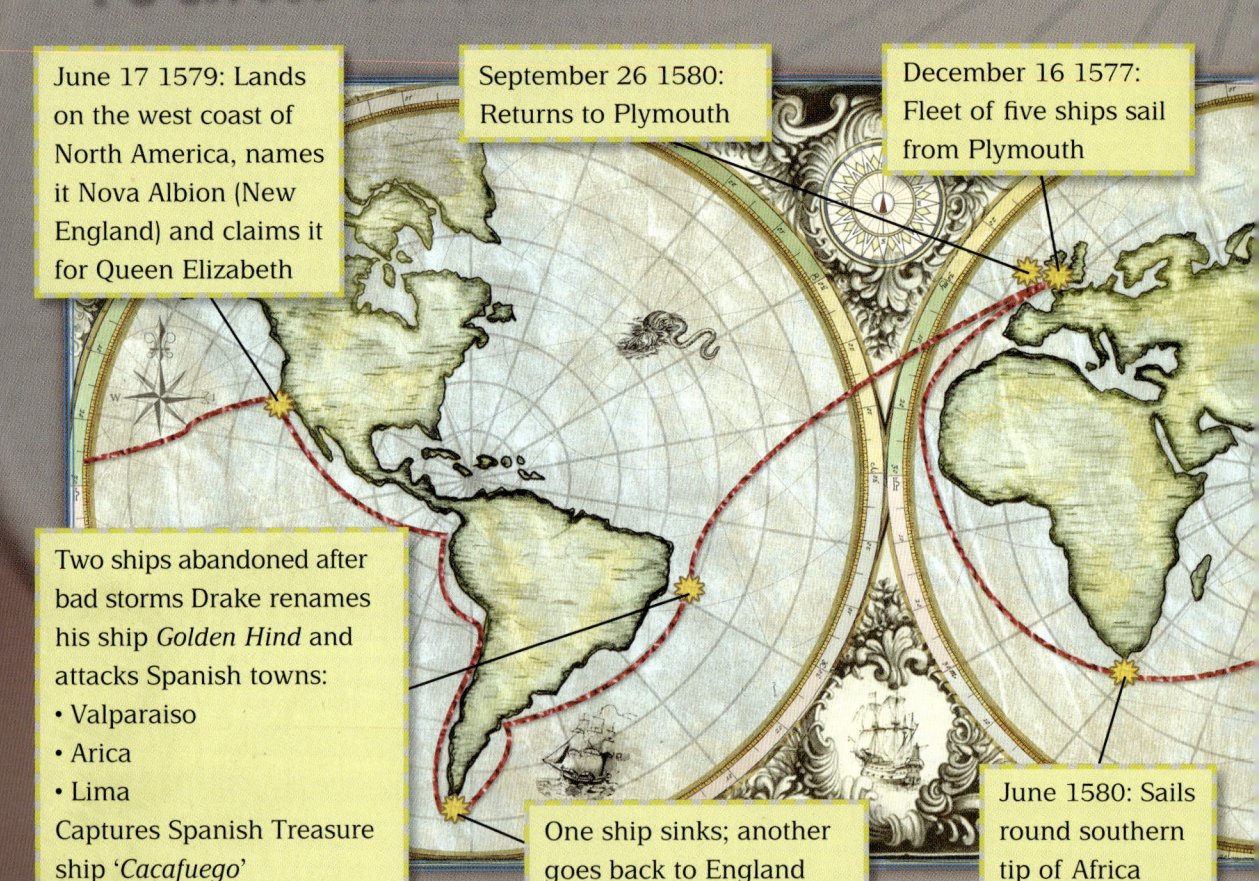

June 17 1579: Lands on the west coast of North America, names it Nova Albion (New England) and claims it for Queen Elizabeth

September 26 1580: Returns to Plymouth

December 16 1577: Fleet of five ships sail from Plymouth

Two ships abandoned after bad storms Drake renames his ship *Golden Hind* and attacks Spanish towns:
- Valparaiso
- Arica
- Lima

Captures Spanish Treasure ship '*Cacafuego*'

One ship sinks; another goes back to England

June 1580: Sails round southern tip of Africa

> The reason for my voyage was to raid Spanish treasure ships. I had secret orders from Queen Elizabeth to steal as much Spanish treasure as my little ships could carry. My route took me all round the world.

The Queen was so pleased she made me *Sir* Francis Drake when I returned.

November 1579: Reaches Spice Isles of the Indies

The treasure Drake brought back was worth £600,000 (approximately £130 million today). That was the same as all the money the Queen got in taxes for a whole year!

9

The legend of Drake's drum

When he was dying, Drake asked that his drum be taken to Buckland Abbey, his home in Devon. He said that if England were ever in danger from an enemy, someone should beat his drum and he would come back to fight.

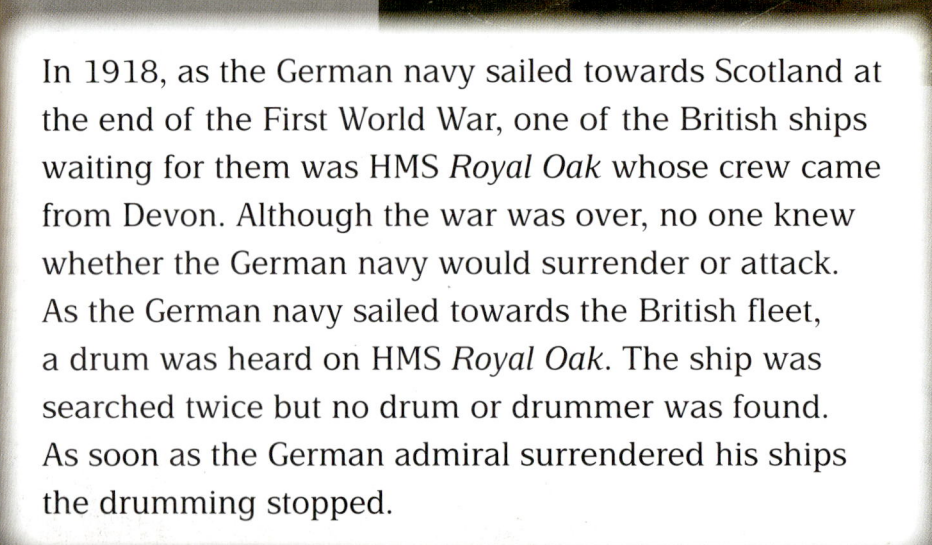

In 1918, as the German navy sailed towards Scotland at the end of the First World War, one of the British ships waiting for them was HMS *Royal Oak* whose crew came from Devon. Although the war was over, no one knew whether the German navy would surrender or attack. As the German navy sailed towards the British fleet, a drum was heard on HMS *Royal Oak*. The ship was searched twice but no drum or drummer was found. As soon as the German admiral surrendered his ships the drumming stopped.

The Outlook

Published Weekly

April 26, 1919

The drum was heard beating in rolls. The ear of the naval officer is attuned to all the noises of his ship in fair weather and foul; it makes no mistakes. All who heard know that they heard the rolling of a drum.

Captain Cook's Endeavour

1768–71

My name is James Cook. I was the officer in charge of HMS *Endeavour*. The first part of the voyage was to take some scientists to Tahiti to watch the planet Venus pass in front of the Sun.

13 July 1771: *Endeavour* arrives back in England

25 August 1768: *Endeavour* leaves England

11 June 1770: Runs aground on Great Barrier Reef

29 April 1770: Passengers go ashore at Botany Bay

19 April 1770: Arrives at east coast of Australia

I also had a packet of sealed orders. My orders told me to carry on sailing south. I was to explore the southern oceans and look for the great continent people believed was there.

I couldn't find it, so instead I sailed to New Zealand and Australia. I made the first accurate maps of New Zealand and the first maps of Eastern Australia.

13 April 1769: Arrives at Tahiti

3 June 1769: Passengers see **transit of Venus**

6 October 1769: Reaches New Zealand

In my day, sailors suffered from a dreadful disease called **scurvy**. I was sure it was caused by the poor food eaten on long voyages. I made my men eat pickled cabbage and citrus fruits, like oranges and limes. Not a single man died of scurvy on the voyage to Australia!

When we came ashore in Australia we saw giant leaping animals. The native people called them kangaroos. Sydney Parkinson, one of the scientists, drew this picture of a kangaroo.

My name is Joseph Banks. I am a plant scientist and I sailed with Cook on the *Endeavour*. I was amazed at what we saw on the islands in the Pacific Ocean and in New Zealand and Australia. I found hundreds of different insects, plants and animals no European had ever seen before. My favourite place was the bay in Australia where we anchored. It had so many new plants we called it **Botany Bay**.

15

South with Shackleton

1914–16

My name is Sir Ernest Shackleton and I led *The Imperial Trans-Antarctic Expedition* which set out in 1914, just as the Great War started. The aim of the expedition was to reach the South Pole and then to travel across the whole of Antarctica.

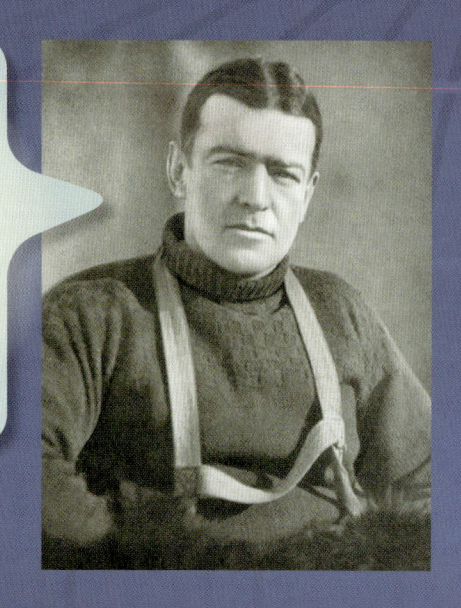

I'm Frank Hurley. I was the photographer on Shackleton's expedition. On the following pages you'll find some photographs I took.

I'd been to Antarctica twice before, but never reached the Pole.

However, before we could reach Antarctica, our ship, *Endurance*, got stuck in ice in the Weddell Sea. We never reached land. Eventually, the weight of the ice crushed the ship and we were stranded on the frozen sea.

Some people say the expedition was a disaster. It would have been if the men from *Endurance* had died on the ice. But they didn't. I brought them all safely back to England.

My crew and I lived on the drifting ice for 15 months. When the ice began to melt, I ordered the men into *Endurance*'s lifeboats and managed to get them all safely to Elephant Island in the South Atlantic.

20 May 1916: Reach whaling village

19 May 1916: Shackleton and two others begin climb across the island to reach the whaling village at Stromness

30 August 1916: Shackleton returns to Elephant Island on the rescue boat *Yelco*. All the men are alive

10 May 1916: *James Caird* lands on the south side of South Georgia

24 April 1916: Shackleton and five others set out in a small boat, the *James Caird*, to get help

15 April 1916: Boats land on Elephant Island

9 April 9 1916: Boats launched into the sea to try to reach Elephant Island

23 December 1915: Expedition begins hauling the boats across the ice

25 October 1915: Shackleton orders crew to "abandon ship"

18

Then six of us took one of the boats and sailed through mountainous seas to the island of South Georgia to get help from the Norwegian whalers who had a village there. But we arrived on the wrong side of the island. Three of us had to climb over the mountains of South Georgia to reach the whalers' village to get help.

5 December 1914: *Endurance* leaves South Georgia, heading for the South Pole

January 1915: *Endurance* trapped in ice

19

"The *Eagle* has landed": Apollo 11

21 July 1969

Between 1947 and 1991, Russia and America were bitter rivals. It was a period known as 'The Cold War'.

Russia launched *Sputnik*, the first artificial **satellite**, in 1957. That started a space race. So when a Russian, Yuri Gagarin, became the first human in space in 1961, the American president John Kennedy promised that an American would land on the Moon by the end of the decade.

Over the next nine years, America spent millions of dollars preparing for the Moon landing. Preparations began with the Mercury project, a small one-person spacecraft. The next stage was Gemini, a two-person craft. Then, the final stage was Apollo – a three-person craft that could land on the Moon.

Although preparations were very thorough, the Moon mission was still very dangerous.

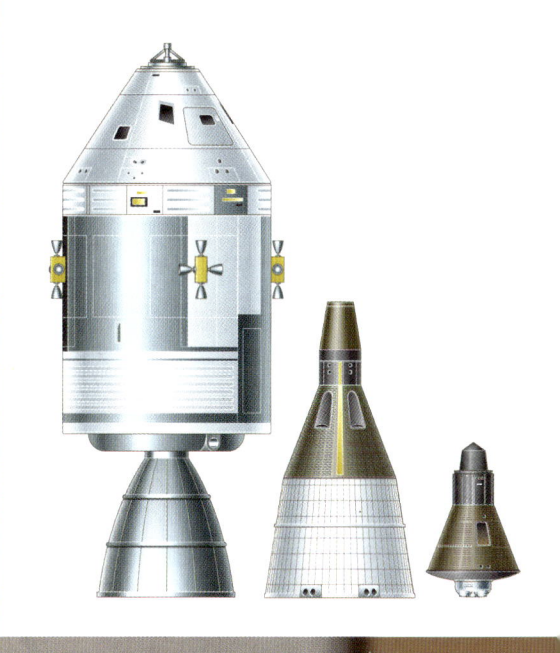

As the countdown started, everyone at Mission Control knew there were many risks.

The Saturn rocket could explode on take-off. If the lunar module was damaged on landing, two astronauts could be stranded on the Moon. The craft could burn up on re-entry into the Earth's atmosphere.

This is Neil Armstrong.
He was commander of Apollo 11.

There were no problems with takeoff, or the flight to the Moon. But as they were coming in to land, Neil and his crewmate, Buzz Aldrin, saw large boulders on the ground. Neil had to steer the lunar module *Eagle* to a safer site. They landed with only 15 seconds of fuel left!

Neil Armstrong was the first human to walk on the Moon. As he stepped from the ladder he said: "It's one small step for a man, one giant leap for mankind."

This is a picture Neil Armstrong took of Buzz Aldrin on the Moon. If you look carefully you might see Neil and the *Eagle* reflected in Buzz's helmet!

Two months later, the crew members made speeches to **Congress**.

This is what Buzz said:
"We walked on the Moon. But the footprints belong to more than the crew of Apollo 11. They were put there by hundreds of thousands of people … people in Government, industry, and universities, the teams and crews that preceded us with Mercury, Gemini, and Apollo."

Glossary, activities and index

Glossary
botany – the study of plants
Congress – the US parliament; like the British parliament, it is made up of two parts – in Congress they are called the House of Representatives and the Senate
satellite – something in orbit around a planet or other body
scurvy – a disease caused by not eating enough foods that contain vitamin C
transit of Venus – when the planet Venus moves in front of the Sun

Other famous explorers
Here are some other explorers who might interest you. Explore your school or local library for books about these and other explorers.

Roald Amundsen and Captain Scott – both men led expeditions in 1912 hoping to be the first to reach the South Pole. Amundsen won, but Scott and his companions died on their journey back from the Pole

Christopher Columbus – sailed west across the Atlantic hoping to reach Asia, but instead, landed on islands off the east coast of America

Ferdinand Magellan – led the first voyage around the world

Marco Polo – an Italian merchant who travelled across Asia to meet the Emperor of China in his palace in Beijing

Index

Aldrin, Buzz   22, 23
Amundsen, Roald   24
Apollo 11   22–23
Armstrong, Neil   22, 23
Banks, Joseph   15
Bjarni   4–5, 6–7
Captain Cook   12–13, 15
Captain Scott   24
Columbus, Christopher   24
Endurance   17, 18
Eric the Red   4
Gagarin, Yuri   20
Golden Hind   8
HMS *Endeavour*   12, 15
HMS *Royal Oak*   10
Hurley, Frank   16
Imperial Trans-Antarctic Expedition   16
knorrs   7
Leif   4–5, 6–7
Magellan, Ferdinand   24
Parkinson, Sydney   14
Polo, Marco   24
Shackleton, Ernest   16–17, 18–19
Sputnik   20